ADVANCED *PRAISE*

"I laughed, I cried, and I was there. Iola Corbett's *Growing up Muslim* is the life story of a child who became a Muslim Woman. The author shares vivid detailed depictions of various landmarks and signature experiences that took place in her hometown, Detroit, Michigan. Iola gives memorable visual images that transport you to the places she describes throughout her story. She speaks to the personal and intimate accounts of listening to and eventually meeting Malcolm X and other leaders of the *Nation of Islam*. Iola shares her transition and subsequent introduction into the *Nation of Islam* and helps the reader to see a genuine connection, not only to the Muslim faith but also to any/all religious faiths as it relates to events and circumstances in this story. A great read that keeps you engaged and anticipating the next chapter. Two Thumbs Up!"

—Tammy Ervin

"History comes alive in Sister Iola's memoir, *Growing Up Muslim*. We are privileged to get this firsthand account from a pioneer of Islam in America. Her story makes me proud as a descendent of a former member of the *Nation of Islam* and as a community historian. Sister Iola's book is a must read. It is a vital piece of Black history, Muslim history, and American history."

—Attorney Zarinah Nadir,
Tempe History Museum Muslim Advisory Board,
MLK Diversity Award Recipient

"*Growing Up Muslim* is the book I have been waiting for! An honest and insightful historical depiction of a young member of the Nation of Islam written in her own words. If you love history you will love her-story!"

—Sabreen Hanifa

Growing UP MUSLIM

Copyright © 2021 by Iola E. Corbett

Growing Up Muslim and the Journey Continues

Published in the United States by Book Power Publishing, an imprint of
Niyah Press, Detroit, Michigan.

www.bookpowerpublishing.com

All rights reserved. This book or parts thereof may not be reproduced in any form, stored in any retrieval system, or transmitted in any form by any means—electronic, mechanical, photocopy, recording, or otherwise—without prior written permission of the publisher, except as provided by United States of America copyright law.

Book Power Publishing books may be purchased for educational, business, or sales promotional use.

For bulk sales, contact the author at: iola.corbett@icloud.com

First Edition

ISBN :978-1-945873-43-0 (Paperback)
ISBN: 978-1-945873-44-7 (Hardback)
ISBN: 978-0-9822215-8-7 (eBook)

CONTENTS

Foreword 11
Preface..15

Chapter One: 1945 To 1955 17
Chapter Two: 1955 To 1965 27
Chapter Three: 1965 To 1975 41
Chapter Four: 1975 To 1985 45
Chapter Five: 1985 To 1995 63
Chapter Six: 1995 To 2005.....................................71
Chapter Seven: 2005 To 2015.................................75
Chapter Eight: 2015 To 2021 83

My Dad: My Dad's Story.......................................87
Down Memory Lane... 101

This book is dedicated to my Mom and Dad, two of the best people I've known in my entire life. If it wasn't for them, I wouldn't even be writing this story.

Growing UP MUSLIM
AND THE JOURNEY CONTINUES

IOLA "AMEEDAH" CORBETT

BOOK POWER PUBLISHING

DETROIT, MICHIGAN

FOREWORD

Wali Muhammad Mosque in Detroit, Michigan, was the first mosque founded by Master Fard Muhammad and the Most Honorable Elijah Muhammad. Many generations have been introduced to the Nation of Islam in this historic mosque and, dating back to the 1930s, it has been transformed into universal practice. In fact, some of the most influential world figures in religion and the human rights struggle for freedom, justice, and equality were produced through the movement that began here.

You have undoubtedly heard of some of the most famous pioneering Muslims produced by the predominately African American Nation of Islam—including the greatest Muhammad Ali, Minister Louis Farrakhan, and the inheritor, Imam W. D. Muhammad. These great men all descended from the tutelage of their leader and teacher the Most Honorable Elijah Muhammad. But seldom do we hear any mention of the many rank- and-file members of the movement, who are affectionately known as the pioneers. These honorable men and women played an intricate part in building one of the most effective socio-religious movements for poor people in world history.

For this reason, I am writing this Foreword for one of these illustrious pioneers who is still in our midst: our beloved sister Ms. Iola Corbett, aka Sister Ameedah. She is a second-generation pioneer who has made significant contributions to our legacy via her experiences as a child growing up Muslim. I am grateful for all the years I have been fortunate enough to benefit from her graceful, well-balanced demeanor and example. For her many admirers, Sister Ameedah has been an excellent example of a committed, selfless hard worker for the Islamic community. I am honored to have spent many days working on special projects with her as an ally in doing G_d's work. To be asked to write this Foreword is an honor in itself; I only hope that it is sufficient for such a wonderful servant of G_d.

In this book, Sister Ameedah shares her life experiences as a young girl growing up in the movement's early years of struggle for survival. She was blessed to have parents who were entrepreneurs in various business ventures as well as staunch supporters of the Honorable Elijah Muhammad. She speaks of working in her family's businesses and recalls memorable experiences of her training in the Muslim Girls Training and General Civilization Class (MGT&GCC). Finally, she shares how her family's businesses afforded her unique opportunities to meet some of the movement's most well-known ministers and soldiers—the men and women of the Nation of Islam. Although most of the first-generation pioneers are deceased, Sister Ameedah and others stand as precious jewels that provide a unique connection to the greatness of our history.

It is my sincere wish that Allah blesses our dear sister with all the success that her soul can handle. And I encourage her readers, especially our youth, to cherish our pioneers and benefit from their narratives while we still have them.

Sincerely,
Imam Tauheed A. Rashad

PREFACE

Over the years, as I shared bits and pieces of my life experiences with family and friends, I became convinced that my life story included lessons that could help others. That's how this book-writing journey began.

In this memoir, I describe how becoming a Muslim at a young age changed my life and the lives of my mom and dad. In recalling my life's story, I share the highs and lows—the good, the bad, and the ugly—and how the lessons I learned changed me. I believe you will find stories here and meet people who will touch your heart.

As a passionate reader, I realized there weren't many stories out there like mine, so I felt a calling to write this book—especially as a way to preserve significant parts of my family's legacy for future generations.

I thank my family for their support, and I am grateful for all the encouragement I received from friends.

CHAPTER ONE

1945 to 1955

421

I n 1945 so many remarkable things were happening. Harry Truman was President. The top news story was the ending of World War II, and our nation rejoiced. You could buy a new Ford for $882 dollars; gas was 21 cents a gallon, and you could buy a pound of bread and a gallon of milk for less than a dollar. (I know that buying bread by the pound sounds funny, but back in the day, sometimes you had to slice your own loaf.)

But on the very last Saturday of June that year, our family celebrated when a new life, my life, was born to Geneva and Jessie Holmes on June 30, 1945: Iola Geneva Holmes. I know it was a Saturday evening because my Aunt Ruby would tell me, "Girl, I could hear you hollering when I got off the Brush Street bus." Aunt Ruby was my dad's only sister, and her family lived with us for as long as I can remember. We lived at 421 Melbourne Street, four houses from Brush Street. Melbourne is on the North

End of Detroit about seven blocks from Grand Boulevard. Now, it's in what they call the New Center Area.

It brings joy to my heart just thinking about 421. It was a big red house, and it was filled with folks. My family was blended. Jessie had a son, Jessie Jr and a daughter, Fannie Mae. She absolutely hated that name, so everyone called her Fran. I didn't meet Fran until I was about 3 years old, and it was love at first sight. I met Jessie Jr a little later. Gee, that's what everyone called my mom, had two sons, William and Paul Agee. Paul was also a Junior, and the boys were always around. Family was always at that big red house. Back then, relatives would come from down South with no lodging, and they would stay with us until they got their own place. At 421, I was surrounded by uncles, aunts, and cousins. I was the baby and spoiled because I was my mom's only little girl.

On our block, there were many families with loads of kids. We were busy with school during the school year and played outside during the summer. One of my more cherished memories is of summer fun with the neighborhood kids. One of the neighbors, Mrs. Ramsure, would take all the kids from our whole block plus kids from the surrounding blocks to Boblo! That was the highlight of the summer. Now, you're probably wondering what Boblo was all about and what made it so special. To start the day, we'd go to the foot of Woodward Avenue and get on the Boblo Boat, which would take us to Boblo Island, a nearby amusement park located on Bois Blanc Island, Ontario. When we arrived, a day of nonstop fun would begin. There was such a variety of great rides, skating, food, and drinks. I can't forget the cotton candy. The last boat returning to Detroit didn't leave until about nine o'clock in the evening. We would return home very tired but so happy.

Other times, my friends and I went to the show for fun. It's called *movies* or *theater* now, but back then, it was "the show," and it was located at the Fisher Theatre on Woodward Avenue. It only cost 25 cents for a movie and candy, but the hardest part was getting my daddy to hand over the quarter. We would walk down Woodward Avenue and go to the show. After the show, we would go underground to the General Motors Building to check out the new cars and then head down the street to the Kresge's Five and Dime, which was located on the Southwest corner of Woodward. We would buy more junk and then walk home. And we were all of about seven years old—My, how times have changed.

I have fond memories of the fall when we would burn leaves in front of the house. Then when it snowed, we kids would have the best snowball fights ever. We would stay outside until we were freezing, go in the house until we warmed up, and then take our positions back in the snow.

One thing we all knew was to be at home when the streetlights came on. This was the perfect time and the perfect block to be a kid. Over the years, my closest childhood friends would play a significant part in my life—even more than they realized. Thank you—Tee, Cliff, and Jeff—for being my devoted childhood friends.

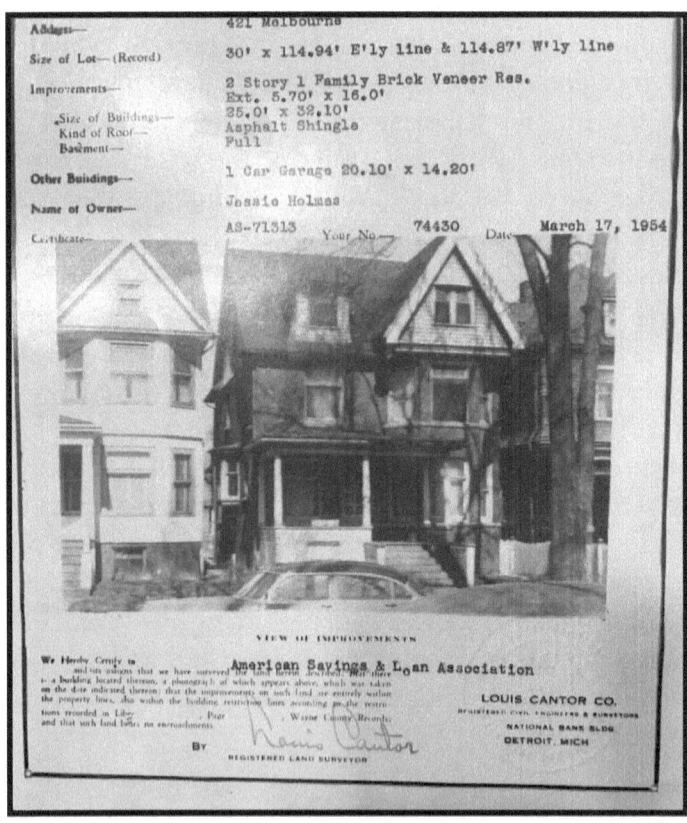

1954 photo of our home at 421 Melbourne Street

421 after many years of improvement inside and out

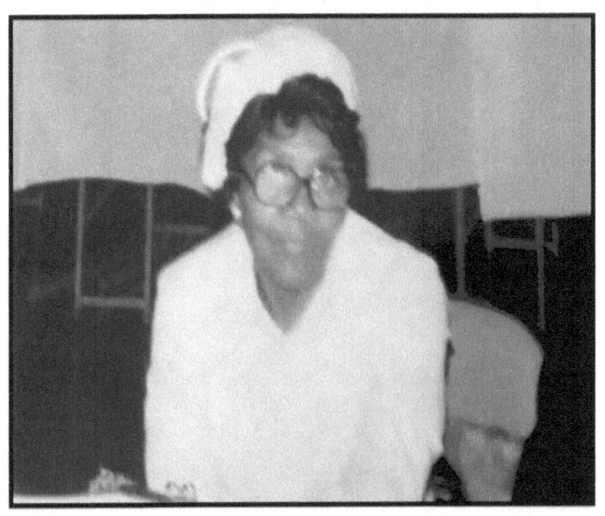

Aunt Ruby, my dad's only sister

My mom pregnant with me

Dad and I

Remembering the Traumatic Crash

In 1948 my family—Mom and Dad (Jessie), Uncle Elijah, two other family members, and I—was returning home from Mississippi. My mom (Gee) was driving, and she fell asleep. The car flipped over three times, and we were all trapped inside. At that moment, we were in Cairo, Illinois. My dad would always say that White people would ride by, stop, look inside our car, and keep going. Finally, someone stopped, broke the windshield, and pulled everyone to safety except me. One of my legs was pinned under the car. Somehow my mother miraculously freed me. I remember her saying she gained strength from somewhere to free her baby.

It's funny how you remember certain things from your childhood. From that night, I remember being on a dark road in a truck with no doors—so scared that I was going to fall out. We were on our way to a country doctor to get my face stitched up. When the windshield was broken, some of the glass cut my face. The country doctor sewed up my face with no painkiller and said if I didn't cry, he'd give me an Almond Joy. It is a wonder I still like Almond Joys today.

I was only three years old when we had the car crash, so I always wondered why Cairo stuck out in my mind. After some investigation, I made a gruesome discovery. In November 1909, William James was lynched in what has been described as the worst lynching in the history of America. It took place in Cairo, Illinois. Almighty God was with us on that lonely road when we had that accident in 1948, and he sent angels to ensure that we would arrive home safely.

My broken leg healed. But growing up with a big scar on my face was a burden for a little girl. The scar was the first thing people saw when they looked at me. Either folks looked at me with pity or the kids were just plain cruel. But my childhood friends came to the rescue: Cliff and Jeff covered the scar and said, "You're pretty!" That gave me confidence for the rest of my life. I'm so happy my friends could see past what was so visible.

And then it gets interesting!

My three-year-old self

Introduction to the Nation of Islam

My mom was not much of a churchgoer but my dad was and he often took me with him. When my sister would take me to church, we went to a Catholic Church, and the services were not very long at all. However, on one warm Sunday, my dad and I went to a different church, not like any we had attended before. It was located around the corner from my dad's barbershop, which was on Russell between Frederick and Kirby streets; this new church was on Frederick Street. The one thing I remembered and couldn't wait to get back to tell my mother was that the preacher said, "The white man was the devil!"

The next time we visited the temple, Malcolm X was speaking. Sister Ella D had invited my dad to this first meeting. He didn't know it, but she had also invited my mom to hear Malcolm. So, they both heard his message at the same time. Dad would often say that message changed his life. So naturally, our lives changed too. The church was called the "temple," and the preacher was called the "minister." They searched everyone when we entered the building and gave us a strange greeting, and we stayed a long, long time.

I learned later that the church was called Temple #1 *Nation of Islam*, and the leader was The Honorable Elijah Muhammad. My dad was completely hooked, and my mom was right on board. They cleaned the house of all pork and pork products. Our relatives didn't know what was going on, but my dad was devoted, and he wanted everyone to be Muslim.

But at first, it was just Mom, Dad, and me. My dad started going to conventions in Chicago for the celebration of Savior's Day each year on February 26th. My mom would cook up all kinds of food, and off we would go. We'd be traveling on Michigan Avenue, a long road from

Detroit to Chicago, for hours. Back then, there was no Interstate 94, and most of the time it was snowing. But it was so exciting. We would meet brothers and sisters from everywhere; the sisters would be wearing their white uniforms, and the brothers were dressed in sharp suits—all coming to the Savior's Day Convention.

When I was about eight years old, we went to New York City, Temple #7 where Malcolm X was the minister. We stayed with Sister Jessie who was Marie Joshua's sister. Sister Joshua and her family were like royalty in Detroit as they had been in the Nation since the thirties. Her daughter was my friend, Baby Gee Marie, and Sister Jessie's daughter was Novene. I had the best time that weekend. I loved New York; it was magical, and it's true the city never sleeps. I'm sure that our love for Malcolm was solidified that convention weekend.

Back home, our lives were becoming Muslim as taught by The Honorable Elijah Muhammad. I wasn't free to rip and run up and down the block anymore; I stayed inside a lot. I don't think I was mad about it; at eight or nine years old, you go along with your parents' program. By then, my life really began to change.

CHAPTER TWO

1955 to 1965

Starting Muslim School and Getting a Job

I graduated from fifth grade at Horton Elementary School and was on my way to middle school. My parents, Bro. Jessie and Sis. Geneva had enrolled me in the University of Islam, the school founded by Sis. Clara Muhammad for Muslim children.

The Temple and school had been moved to a theater building at 5401 John C Lodge; the building was plenty big enough to house both the temple and the school. So, on the first Monday in September 1955, Bro. Lenton, the school bus driver picked me up. I was one of the first on the bus. I didn't realize it would be such a long ride, but the school provided transportation for all the students who needed it, and our first stop was Roseville, Michigan, which was a whole 19 miles away. The next stop was Mount Clemens, Michigan, which was 24 miles from Detroit. The parents were determined to give their children a Muslim education. By the time we finally made it to school, I was tired of that bus. Also Bro. Lenton was a strict bus driver; he was nice, but you would not be cuttin' up on his bus. There would be no singing "The Wheels on the Bus Go Round." I was already nervous, so I was on my best behavior.

Something else changed around this time. We moved from 421. At that point, that was just about the saddest thing that could have happened to me. I missed my home, my room; heck, I missed my friends. Now I was in a new school and a new home. Our new home was an apartment above my dad's barbershop and my mom's restaurant. The new addresses were on Russell Street: 5329 for home, 5331 for the restaurant, and 5331 for the barbershop. To give you an idea of where we were located: Russell was about three blocks east of Hastings Street better known as Black Bottom. I just know that the area had loads of Black people and a lot of Black shops.

The lucky thing is my Aunt Ruby and Uncle Abraham stayed in the house at 421, so all was not lost forever.

I felt lonely in the new living space but not in the restaurant, which was known as *Shabazz*. I would go to school four days a week and I worked every day after school. Tuesday was our recreation day. There was always something happening at the *Shabazz*. Dorranna Ali worked in the restaurant during the day, and Roscoe Jr. and I would work after school. Roscoe was part of the Muhammad family; his grandma was the Honorable Elijah Muhammad's sister. We had plenty of customers, and my mom was the best cook in the entire world. Our place had become a gathering place for the Muslims at Temple #1. My mom had made friends with all the sisters at the temple—and I'm talking about sisters who had been in the temple from when it started in 1930, so she had a wealth of information. The sisters told her about collecting pennies and putting them together to establish the first temple in Detroit. They were proud of their accomplishments as each change of location had been a tremendous improvement.

The minister at Temple #1 was Lemuel Hassan. I remember him being a very powerful speaker. Temple meetings were held on Wednesday and Friday nights, and on Sundays during the day. We were there most nights. Monday was the night for the F.O.I. (Fruit of Islam) men only meetings. Thursday night was the meetings for MGT & GCC (Muslim Girls Training and General Civilization Class) for women and girls only. Of course, I was there every time, learning the skills for being a successful homemaker, sewing and cooking. After these meetings, the *Shabazz* would be busy. I was always around older adults, both at home and at school.

The buzz around the temple was that Minister Lemuel was ready to retire and that we would soon need a new minister. So, guess who the Honorable Elijah sent to Detroit to oversee the selection. Yep, he sent Malcolm X.

One day after getting home from school, Roscoe and I were feeding the jukebox and enjoying the music when who did we see coming through the door? Mr. Malcom X himself. I was nervous, excited, embarrassed, and happy—all at the same time. I had seen him on the rostrum and at conventions, but there he was alive and in living color. He was very tall, light-skinned with sandy hair, and a huge smile. Did I say handsome? I was eleven, but I knew handsome. And for the next 30 days, he came every day and ate dinner with my dad. Of course, I was the waitress, and my mom was the cook in the kitchen.

In the evening, the brothers—mainly single men—would come to hear more wisdom from Malcolm. One time he said, "Iola, get the Bible." I turned to that section that says, "It's better to marry than to burn" (1 Corinthians 7:9 KJV). These interactions happened two or three times a week. His presence was great for business, and I'd get loads of tips. Malcolm came in one day and asked me what I did with my tips. I had to be honest. I said I put them in the jukebox, but after my talk with him, I did better with my tips.

At the end of those 30 days, we had a new minister. He was Brother Wilfred X, Malcolm's oldest brother. With Bro. Malcolm coming to Detroit so often, everybody who was anybody came to the *Shabazz*—even Louis X (aka Louis Farrakhan) and his wife. I wish we had had camera phones back then.

Thinking back, I believe I got to do lots of things because of Malcolm X. For instance, I wasn't afraid to speak to a crowd, so Minister Wilfred asked if I could go to cities around Michigan and speak to believers about what being a Muslim meant to me. These folks didn't have a temple, so the meetings were held in their homes. Once, I spoke at a Savior's Day Convention in Chicago; I was dressed in my white uniform representing the junior MGT & GCC! These were exciting times for a very young girl.

Me and the jukebox

Me at 12 years old

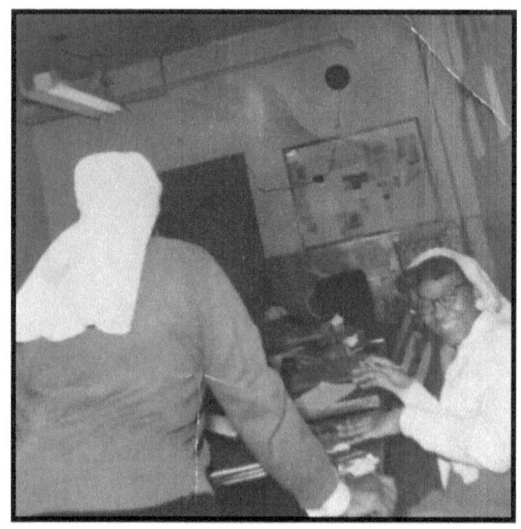

Me in class at the University of Islam

Willie and I on John C. Lodge

The Temple of Islam Moves Again

The temple and school moved to 11529 Linwood Avenue, and it was an absolutely beautiful place. We had real classrooms, office space, and a large auditorium. The facility was just right for our growing Muslim family. Bro. Ernest (Imam Abdul Ghani) was my teacher. I have so many fond memories of being taught in that space at that time.

Malcolm X was instrumental in us moving to this new location. I remember the last three times I saw Malcolm up close and personal.

Remember I told you about Novene in New York. Well, by now she was one of the Honorable Elijah Muhammad's secretaries. Baby Gee and I were in Chicago to help her sister, Minnie, serve dinner to some of the ministers. Minnie was married to John Ali who was the Secretary to the *Nation of Islam*. I got to serve Malcolm once again; we kept running into each other.

That trip was some adventure. Baby Gee and I took the L-train to the Honorable Elijah Muhammad's house—I think that had to be about 1957 or 1958. Novene told us to knock on the back door, but by the time we got there, it was dark! There we were: two teens at the back door of the Honorable Elijah's house. Well, we were scared to death, but we got in and were escorted into his beautiful living room. We met Sis. Clara Muhammad, and soon we were in limousines off to see *A White Man's Heaven Is a Black Man's Hell*, starring none other than Louis X. Can you believe it? It was a grand evening, and we had front row seats. I often marvel that I have had such an amazing journey with the Nation.

The next time I saw Malcom up close was at the *Shabazz*. We had moved from Russell Street further east to East Forest and Burns Streets. Again, my dad's business was next door; this time, he was managing Ray's Barber Shop. Raymond Cantrell was the owner; he later became the owner of Cantrell's Funeral Home. Anyway, one evening no one was in the restaurant except family, and who should walk in? Yep, Malcolm X. He stopped in to introduce his wife, Sis. Betty and his little girl who was still crawling. I will never forget my mom and dad's reaction. It was touching now that I'm older to think that he wanted my family to meet his family. That's the kind of man he was.

The last time I saw Malcolm, he was in town for one of our fundraisers. And when he was in town, everybody came to the *Shabazz* because they knew he was going to show up. He came through with his brother, Minister Wilfred. Malcolm didn't stay long, and I didn't know then that would be the very last time I would see him.

Temple meeting at 11529 Linwood Avenue

Crowd waiting for Malcolm X to come
Public School, Marriage, Graduation,
and Separation—in That Order

The University of Islam didn't offer high school, so after ninth grade, I was off to public school. I loved business, so I enrolled at Commerce High School; back then, it was connected to Cass Tech (formally, Cass Technical High School). To put it mildly, my transition was a cultural shock. I'd never been in a school that big before. And you could tell I'd been very sheltered, so I didn't do very well while I was there. The environment was totally different from the University of Islam. When summer came, I knew I didn't want to go back. I volunteered at the University that summer, helping Sis. Ozetta with the little kids. Once again, a bus would pick me up, and off we'd go on our route until we got to school. I was back home again.

In September 1961, I started at Northern High School, and . . . Bam, it was different, but I was comfortable. By this time, we had moved back to 421, and life was good. I did well at Northern; I still got my business classes in, but my favorite subject was history. One of my classmates was Melvin Franklin; this was before he became one of the *Temptations!*

During my last year at Northern, I married John Wesley Ervin. I was sixteen when I got to know John in the *Shabazz* on Russell Street and on East Forest Street. I really think I just wanted to leave home. I say that because I really did not know what I was doing. I got married in August and by November, we were separated, and I was back at 421, finishing up my last months before my high school graduation in January. (At my high school, there were two graduating classes—the 12A class graduated in June, and the 12B class graduated in January.)

In November, I was two months pregnant. I was totally depressed: John and I were separated, I was pregnant, and I was living back home with my parents. So much for leaving home. I thought my only option was to go back to John and try to make it work. That's what I did. I had a son, John

Jr., and two years later, Tonda was born. I was busy being a mom and a wife, but I never felt the wife part.

I attended the temple and some MGT classes, and I was in plays written and directed by Sis. Burnsteen Muhammad. Her husband was John Muhammad, brother of Elijah Muhammad. Once again, I was in front of a crowd and unafraid. That was so much fun, and it allowed me to be away from my home life. I was about twenty years old.

My eighth-grade graduation was held in Chicago at Temple #2.

Graduating class of 8th and 12th graders at Temple #2

Graduation from Northern High School, 1962

Malcom X Killed

On Sunday, February 21, 1965, I was at Sis. Franceno's house. We would often get together and cook or sew. That Sunday, we were cooking. Her husband, Bro. Lenton (my first bus driver) and my husband had gone to the Savior's Day Convention in Chicago. So, we were enjoying our day; my two kids and her three boys were having a good visit. We needed something from the store, so I walked up the block to get the items that we needed. We probably needed cranberry sauce, which is my favorite with dressing. Anyway, while I was in the store, it was announced on the radio that Malcolm X had been shot. I felt horrible and was in disbelief.

Who would kill Malcolm? I knew he was not in the *Nation of Islam* anymore, and some folks were saying bad things about him, but to kill him seemed unbelievable. It goes without saying that we finished dinner that evening only because we had hungry children. Franceno and I were not interested in food. It was late when our husbands made it back home, and everyone was just numb.

My dad was always quiet about Malcolm. I know he had a lot of thoughts about the events and all the talk going on around the temple, but he never engaged. And the love for Mr. X remained in my dad's heart until his death. May Allah forgive their missteps and grant them Paradise, Ameen.

It was many years later that I felt comfortable expressing my love for Malcolm and sharing what a big part of my childhood he had been. It's funny how people have to die before you can acknowledge their contributions. In all, Allah knows best.

Our children are under the sink!
Roderick, Tonda, John Jr, Lenton Jr, and Darrick

Some of the "kids under the sink" and their brothers: Marvin, Lenton Jr, Me, Gerrard, Darrick, and Roderick—The Muhammad Men

CHAPTER THREE

1965 to 1975

More Kids and a Miserable Life

By the time I was twenty-six years old, I had five children: two boys (John Jr and Gamal) and three girls (Tonda, Melanie, and Jamillah). I can't begin to tell you how unhappy I was. I lived in a beautiful house in a neighborhood you wouldn't believe, and I had everything you could imagine. But I learned that things don't make you happy. And putting these words on paper, I also know that having a young girl around a lot of adult males is not a good thing. You grow up too fast, and you miss out on your childhood. You get to be a mom before you know who you really are.

I found out who I could be on a very extended trip to Nashville, Tennessee. I stayed with my husband's stepfamily, and I had the best time of my life. It was not my choice to go or to stay, but I ended up there for almost three months—just my two small daughters and me.

Our niece, Veronica, was getting married, so I made dresses—one for the mother of the bride and three for my girls and me. I cooked and helped out whenever I could. I got to see a real marriage with a man who adored his wife. I was free, and I realized life was passing me by. I could have stayed if it wasn't for the fact that my other three children had been dropped off at my mother's house. The in-laws were so kind to me, and this visit came at a time when I really needed it.

By the time I returned home, my mind was made up!

Baby Jamillah, Melanie, Gamal, Tonda, and John Jr

My husband John and I

CHAPTER FOUR

1975 to 1985

Divorced and a New Home

So, in 1975, I found myself without a home, with five kids, no job, and just a high school diploma. I did manage to get away from the marriage with some cash, and I mean "get away." My mom and dad took us in once again. But I couldn't remain there forever. I called my brother Paul. He and I mainly saw each other on holidays, but this was an emergency, and I was asking him for the biggest favor. So, I asked him, "Do you want to buy a house?" With no hesitation, he said, "Sure." I had money but no credit, so the plan was for him to put the house in his name, and I would make the payments. I started looking for the right house, and I found a four-bedroom bungalow at 16510 Fenmore Street on the northwest side of Detroit. It was about five minutes from where John and I lived on West Outer Drive.

In July 1975, I was in court and my divorce was being finalized. It was bittersweet; I cried all the way home—not because the marriage was over but because I felt I had wasted fourteen years of my life. The only things I wanted to walk away with were my children and the **car**! With five little people, you needed transportation. Dad also gave me a car; it was an Opal wagon, but it was a stick shift. Dad tried to teach me how to drive it, but we were not having any success. Man, that car sat in front of the house for weeks.

One day, I was determined to get the hang of that stick shift. It was garbage pickup day, and back then, men actually picked up the garbage. A man called out, "Lady, what are you doing?" I explained it to him, and he said, "Come on!" We drove around a few blocks, and when we returned, I had mastered that tiny Opal. I was so proud, and my dad was beaming; he figured all ladies needed to know how to drive a stick shift. He would say, "Anybody can drive an automatic."

Just what will I master next—?

16510 Fenmore in 1975

That's the Opal.

Work Life Begins

I was getting into the routine of being a single mother. We loved our house! The street was beautiful, and the children were getting acquainted with our neighbors. Mind you, I moved right between Mr. and Mrs. Hinneman and Mr. and Mrs. Adamson. They were two of the nicest Caucasian couples you'd ever want to meet. And they had no children. So, this was a real game changer. After many years, the Adamsons moved. Our family got a chance to help care for Mrs. Hinneman when it became hard for her to take care of herself. Soon, some of her family came and took her away.

    Soon after we settled in, I had to start thinking about income. There was child support, but that was meager and not enough. I was in Minnesota Fabrics one day and saw a Help Wanted sign! I applied and got the job. You had to know how to sew. *"Thank you, MGT and Franceno."* I was plenty qualified. I worked the afternoon shift, but that was very challenging because my kids were home alone. Thank God for my daughter, Tonda, who took care of everything.

My youngest, Jamillah, was about to go to kindergarten, and the Muslim school had closed. Oh, my goodness, I was in a panic. It turned out okay. I became a noon hour aide, and that allowed me to keep an eye on my three kids at Cooke School.

Soon, another position became available in the Reading and Math Lab, and I got that job. I was working days at school and evenings at Minnesota Fabrics just to make ends meet. I really had amazing children because they were raising themselves with help from family and friends and the best neighbors.

I attended the temple when I could, but with two jobs and five children, that was on the back burner. And I was wondering, *How could Allah let this happen to me? I am a good person, I'm a good mother, and I was a good wife.* I watched my parents care about each other all my life. I never heard harsh words. I asked myself, *What happened?*

I got my answer from an unlikely source: My childhood sweetheart. I was at the Mosque one Sunday afternoon when I saw this brother who looked so familiar, but after the service I didn't see him, so I headed for my car. As I walked down Linwood Avenue, there he was, more handsome than ever. I always thought he was my soul mate.

He was Maurice Walker; I had met him on Russell Street when I was eleven, and I knew I was in love. I think he was seventeen. It lasted a few months, and his dad came from Pittsburg and took him home because he wasn't doing so well living with his mom.

The next time I saw him was at an Islamic Convention in Pittsburgh, and he had the nerve to have a wife. I hadn't seen or heard from him since. And there he stood in front of me. We chatted for a few minutes, and I gave him my phone number. No cell phones back then.

He came over to meet my family, and now his name was Saud Shabazz. He would stay with my kids when I was at work and leave before I got home. I always appreciated that my family was safe whenever he was around.

But the advice he shared that day was for my soul. He told me I couldn't blame Allah. I had choices, and my choice had been to stay in a terrible situation. I needed to accept the part that I played and live a better life going forward. And that's what I tried to do. And no, we didn't get a second chance. Then . . .

IOLA "AMEEDAH" CORBETT

Working at Cooke Elementary School

Working at Cooke Elementary School

Maurice Walker

Saud Shabazz aka Maurice Walker

Wallace D. Muhammad

Things were really changing at the temple/mosque. And in 1975, the unbelievable happened. The Honorable Elijah Muhammad passed away; it was shocking because I think we really believed he was not going to die. Just saying that seems strange today. I was at the beauty shop that day, and my mom was on her way to the convention in Chicago. My dad was alone, and I wanted to talk to him. He sounded sad—another hero of his gone. We wondered what was going to happen to the *Nation of Islam*.

I thought back to the time when I had met Elijah Muhammad in the *Shabazz*. His niece, Lovella Muhammad, worked for my parents. She was a jewel in our lives—very nice and no nonsense. And I'm sure that's how we got that visit from Elijah Muhammad. So, you know my mom and dad were nervous wrecks, but he was kind; he offered some suggestions and left us with so much pride.

Our leader had passed, and we were all feeling sad. Then I attended the convention on a nationwide hookup, and I left feeling so much better. By the end of the meeting, Wallace D Muhammad took over for his father, and it was with overwhelming approval.

Imam, as I always called him, was taking no prisoners; things were changing rapidly. We were praying differently and dressing differently—always modest but no uniforms. And there was no one always looking over your shoulders, just Allah.

The Imam guided us to worldwide Islam, which was a totally different doctrine from his dad. My mom and dad were on board again. I had always been led to believe that Wallace was the next in line to be the leader, but he was out of the Nation a lot, and I began to understand why. He led us straight to: *There is no God but Allah and Prophet Muhammad, peace be upon him, from 1400 years ago is His Last Messenger. All praise is due to Allah. (A.P.I.D.T.A.)*

At Mosque #1, people were changing their names, and they were making picture IDs with their Arabic names. My mom and dad changed their names, and they were so proud. Before, everybody just had an X, so I was Iola X; my favorite friend Saud chose Ameedah for me. I really liked it, but it meant "one who offers support," and it seemed that's all I did—support, support, support, so I had an attitude. And I knew my mother would never call me anything but what she named me. But sometimes you have to grow, and I did and realized that's what I do: **support**! I also said, *I'll just take my husband's last name.* I got an ID with Ameedah Shabazz on it.

By the way, at that time Bro. Philbert Omar was the Imam at No. 1. He was another one of Malcolm's brothers. So far, I've met everybody connected to the leadership of the Nation.

On my way to see Imam Muhammad

Waiting for Saud to pick me up

Life at DECCO

DECCO was the Detroit Coil Company, and God blessed me to be hired there in October 1978. I really needed a job that paid more money and would not require me to work day and night. DECCO was a small manufacturing company that made industrial solenoids; it was located in Ferndale, Michigan, just north of Detroit. I can say now, it was the best place in the world for a woman to work. DECCO was family-owned, and it was a union shop!

When I started, DECCO employed about one hundred sixteen people, and I was at the bottom of the seniority list but so grateful to be there. It was a great opportunity—so many firsts for me working there. The workforce was diverse, and the majority were women. I think that's why it was so perfect. There were men, but they were mainly general factory workers who did the heavy lifting. The women were builders; they ran the ovens and some machines. I worked in the assembly department, stockroom, and shipping and receiving. And the front office was just a door away. I started off stacking; that's the first part to the solenoid. That probably was my least favorite job, and I was not very good at that. But after a short time, I moved to the light machines and the ovens. After a few months, they had a layoff, and I remember seeing my name at the bottom of the seniority list. I was the first to go.

After this happened a couple of times, I started learning about unions. I went to meetings and educated myself on the benefits that we enjoy as union members. In January 1979 a few new people were hired, and in walks this handsome young man, Clifton Corbett Jr., and my life changed forever!

Coworkers at DECCO, dressed in red celebrating Heart Health Month

My last day at DECCO (2007)

The front offices at DECCO

Clifton and I

Clifton E. Corbett, Jessica's dad

Marriage in 1981 and . . .

Yes, that's just what happened! After meeting and getting to know each other, sparks were flying, and I was ready to try it again. Man, when you have been so unhappy and someone comes along and is really good to you, it makes all the difference in the world. We came from very different backgrounds, and we had some bumps, but we really liked each other. And Clift's family was the very best to me, and to this day, they are still family. We were together for over two years and then—Jess!!

Jessica was born in 1982, and the rest is history. When she was born, Clift was in a major car accident and couldn't be present for her birth, but we were happy, and so were her five siblings.

We hit another snag and couldn't recover, so we separated. I'm sure our backgrounds had a lot to do with our breakup. We worked together every day until he got sick, and we remained the best of friends.

Leadership Opportunities in My Union Local

By then, there were people below me in seniority, and I didn't get the layoffs. I also learned that if you were a steward, you had top seniority and would be the last one to be laid off. I became active in Local Lodge 82, and I became the steward at the shop. Then I became Local Lodge secretary, then treasurer, and vice president. Finally, I became the first woman—the first Black woman— president of Local Lodge 82 of the IAMAW. These positions afforded me great access to training at the headquarters in Maryland, just outside Washington, DC, and all you had to do was participate. I was chosen for a Blue-Ribbon Commission. We went across the United States setting up town hall meetings, listening to union members' suggestions and complaints. We went as far as Halifax, Nova Scotia. Wow! What an experience.

Union leaders on a training trip

I didn't tell you that at the time, our union membership consisted mainly of White men and hardly any women and only a few Black men. I tell you this to let you know that I was always treated with respect. And in all our travels, they looked out for me wherever we went.

But I was not prepared for what happened next!

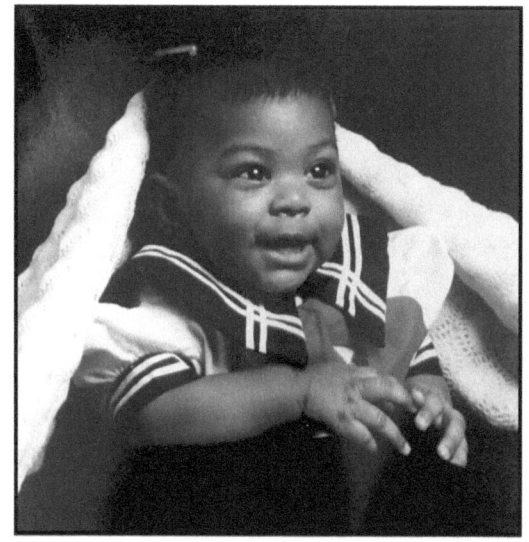

Jessica

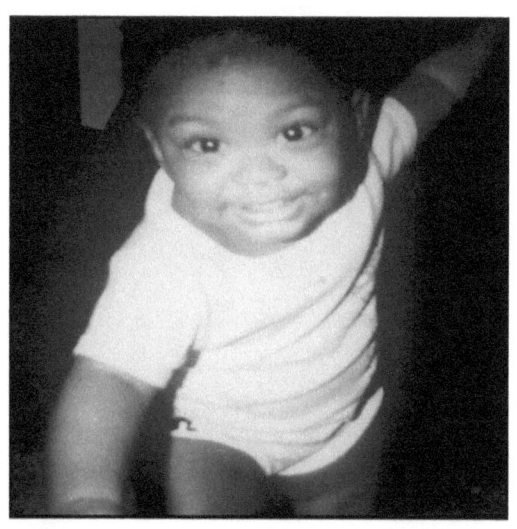

Jessica

CHAPTER FIVE

1985 to 1995

Mu-min Passes Away

Remember I told you earlier about my childhood sweetheart? Well, here we go again. My dad was beginning to get sick, and that was kind of shocking because he was always well—always at the barbershop, watching baseball on his tiny TV. I think that's why I like baseball today. With baseball, you could read your book, you could crochet and still, when the excitement begins, you could be all in and enjoying the game. At home, Mu-min would play his guitar and he'd sing. Just thinking about it, I can see why mom was all in. Besides all that, he was very handsome. So, when he ended up in the hospital, we were alarmed.

When I got home from visiting him one day, the kids gave me a message that Bro. Shabazz had called. I hadn't heard from him in a long while. When he called back, we caught up on our lives, and I told him about my dad. He said he wanted to visit, so I took him to the hospital. My dad had introduced him to the *Nation of Islam* when he was a teenager, and they had a great time going down memory lane. And Mu-min was so happy that they both were on the path of Al Islam. Saud was family, and I knew my dad loved him.

My dad's hospital stay wasn't very long, and he seemed to be doing good. And once again, my childhood crush had come and gone.

What's more, things with my dad were not what they seemed. The one thing Mu-min had never shared with us was that he had been diagnosed with prostate cancer, and by that time, his health was really failing. Soon, he was in the hospital again, but we expected him to recover.

On October 30th, I told my mom I was going to work and that I would come the next day, and we both would go and visit Dad at the hospital. DECCO was closing the nightshift, and I didn't have enough seniority to go on days. That would be my last day until I really didn't know when. At work that night, October 30, 1987, I got the call that my dad had passed, and my mom was at the hospital alone.

The next day we were at Cantrell's Funeral Home in a situation that we weren't prepared for. We didn't know anything about putting anyone in the ground. My mom kept asking, "How much do you spend? How much do you spend?" I'm like, "I do not know." As soon as she said that a light bulb came on. Mu-min had always said, "Don't put your money in the ground." So that was settled.

On the third day, we had a Janazah service for my dad, and it was beautiful. It was the first one I had witnessed and participated in, and it was just what my dad had requested. Imam Meekkaaeel Abdullah was the Imam at Masjid Wali Muhammad at the time, and his words were so comforting, and they made my family feel so at ease. It was also their first Janazah experience. My sister, Fran commented that it was the best funeral she'd ever been to. She was Catholic, and their services were very different. She'd also experienced other Christian funerals, and Dad's was so different. She had also invited her priest, Father Thomas, and I would see him often over the years. We weren't extremely sad at the service and that was an ease for my mom.

Mu-min was a very quiet and gentle man whose feelings ran very deep. He loved Gee, my mom; he adored his family and was devoted to his faith. He lived by this principle: "If you don't have anything nice to say, don't say anything."

With Mu-min gone, *what's going to happen at 421 without him?*

Bro Jessie

IOLA "AMEEDAH" CORBETT

Bro Jessie

Mu-min Abdullah

Mubarak

When Mu-min passed away, I became more active in my mom's life. She was always doing things at the masjid, and my "brother from another mother," Ibrahim, was always close by. And my children were a blessing as far as helping out whenever needed. And Mom's door and kitchen were always open. I wasn't attending the masjid very often, but I did attend when I could, and my mom kept me up on all the happenings in the community. She started talking about this new Imam at the masjid and said I should come to check him out. So, one Sunday I picked her up and off we went. He was a young man—very sharp and dynamic in his presentation. After I took Mom home and we talked about what I had heard, I had a renewed connection to my faith, and I wanted to become more involved.

The new Imam was explaining Imam Muhammad's teaching so plainly, connecting us to worldwide Islam but still within our own community. He reminded me of Malcolm X with his delivery. I worked afternoons, so I started volunteering in the office at the masjid in the mornings a few days a week. I had worked in the office when I was growing up, so it was familiar to me. I attended lectures by Imam Muhammad and by then, we were doing Ramadan with Muslims around the world. And that time, Ramadan was celebrated during the heat of summer. I was trying to fast even though I had to work; it was not easy, but I made it through. However, I couldn't get off work to attend Jumu'ah. So, I spent my Sundays at the masjid. It would be packed; loads of brothers and sisters would come out. I attributed the response to the new Imam. It seemed to me that everyone was happy to be there, and I busied myself with community things whenever I could.

We had a fundraiser, and I don't know how I managed to get there, but I was sitting at the Imam's table next to his daughter, Bakirah. We were chatting, and I happened to tell her how handsome her dad was each time I would see him at Saviour's Day. I think I might have said that he was "fine." She pulled out a picture of him from back in the day and turned to the Imam and said, "Sister Ameedah said you were fine back in the day!" I wanted to get under the table, but I just smiled. He was very gracious, and Imam Mubarak just laughed because he knew I had a crush on the Imam when he was single.

And you know I had more than enough family stuff. I had my mom; I had a nine-year-old, a college student, four grown children, and three grandchildren. Imam Mubarak was there for a few years, and he made a big impression on my understanding of Al Islam. The atmosphere was not the same to me when he left, but in all things, Allah Knows Best!

So, who would be the next Imam at Masjid Wali Muhammad?

Mubarak and Sheriff Benny Napoleon

Members at Masjid Wali Muhammad

Strong Believing Men

CHAPTER SIX

1995 to 2005

Balancing Act

A lot of these years were spent keeping up with Imam Muhammad. He came to Detroit often back in the day, and that was always exciting. I had three sisters—Maryam, Halimah, and Vickie—and we would travel together to different conventions to hear the Imam.

Maryam was the best ballroom dancer in the city of Detroit, so we would go dancing, and I mainly would watch her dance.

My family was working, and two children had left the state. Jamillah was north of Chicago and Melanie was in LA. Guess who lived in Los Angeles? Yep! Bro. Shabazz. So, Melanie did have someone like family if she needed him. He and I would talk over the years, and I knew that I would see him at some point. I visited LA a couple of times and saw Saud each time. I knew by now that he and I would be friends until death. And we were.

At the union, my Local 82 merged with the larger Local 698. Local 82 had been one of the oldest locals in the International Association of Machinists (IAM), and now it was no more. So, I got busy working with Local 698. I became Chairman of the Community Services Committee. This position afforded me the opportunity to go back to our training school. Human Rights and Community Services were some of the courses they offered. The Human Rights classes afforded me the opportunity to visit the halls of Congress and speak with our representatives. We could discuss any issue that was important to our members and community.

IAM believed in training its members; usually, courses lasted for a week, and you had nothing to do but go to class, study your assignments, do your homework; they provided everything else. After class and dinner, you got a chance to network with union members from all over the country and Canada. It was a privilege to be chosen to attend—this was an example of our union dues at work.

On the home front, we worked hard serving our members, their families, and the community. We did things such as paint homes and prepare food baskets for Thanksgiving and Christmas. We built ramps for the handicapped and collected items for the homeless. We visited nursing homes. We did these activities in association with the Metro AFL-CIO. We were a group of different unions who worked together to help Wayne, Oakland, and Macomb County members. This was an example of unions at their best, and I was proud to contribute whatever I could.

After I retired, I became active in the Community Services at Masjid Wali Muhammad; Community services has been a mover and shaker for many years at the masjid. My favorite part is the fourth Sunday Breakfast. It's a staple in our community with good food and great company. Sister Tauheedah Beyah is our chairperson.

Bro. Shabazz

CHAPTER SEVEN

2005 to 2015

Lots of Loss and Life

It had been years since Mu-min passed, and our family rallied to spend as much time as we could with my mom for all birthdays, all holidays, and especially Thanksgiving. All the family would get together and cook, laugh, and eat. For a long time, we would celebrate EID. We would pull names, and the gifts would be flowing. *Wakeelah* (mom) would be so excited by any little thing that you gave her; I can still hear her squeal of excitement.

I was spending a lot of time at 421, and I'm so thankful for Sis. Dorothy who took such good care of my mom. She made my life easier. I didn't have to worry about the day-to-day while I was at work. Mom was pretty much wheelchair-bound, but she could be alone for short periods of time. My son, John, moved in, not so much to provide care but mostly just to be there for Mom.

After a while, Dorothy had to have surgery and I was asking myself, *What am I going to do?* I was a wreck, worrying about Mom while I was at work. Bro. Ash Shakoor needed some living arrangements, so it helped out to have him there, but we still had no physical care until I got off work. That was not working out at all.

God is so merciful. My former coworker, Mercedes Conway, came to my rescue. She agreed to help. The very day she came by, Mom had a doctor's visit. After the examination the doctor told us that Mom needed a better quality of care; he wanted her to go to the hospital for about a week. And then I would need to find a nursing home. Writing this brings tears to my eyes. That was the hardest decision I've ever had to make. Everybody always says, "I'd never put my parents in a home." But I found it was the best decision for her. The facility was within walking distance for me, and she was never sad. I went to visit after work every day, my sister Fran, my kids, and my grandkids visited her often. Other Muslim sisters were also in the same facility. I even saw Malcolm's younger brother Wesley there. So, when I was visiting, Muslims were always there. I do know that if you see about your loved ones in the nursing home, the staff will take care of them. My son, John, would bring gifts to the staff on her floor just to say thank you for taking care of my grandmother. I learned from this; if I ever need it, I just want my friends and family to come see about me.

For years, it had been just Fran, my mom, and I; my brothers passed away years before. William Agee died in Florida; his death was a homicide under very suspicious circumstances, but we never got any answers. They found Jessie Holmes Jr. dead at his home. Paul Agee Jr. had a heart attack in his car. These were my mom's two sons and my dad's only son.

February 2006

Detroit was buzzing. We were hosting the Super Bowl at Ford Field. Once again Mr. Saud Shabazz was coming to town. Saud was from Pittsburg, and the Steelers were playing in the Super Bowl. I always remember him being a super football fan, and he looked and sounded excited. Not so much me. He saw his home team win the Super Bowl. We visited family and friends, and my son, Gamal, made dinner for him. That connected to my heart. He was so good to my kids whenever he was around, and they remembered. Saud was in the D for about a week, and when I dropped him off at the airport, I had a feeling that it would be my last time seeing him, and indeed it was.

Later in 2006, Melanie called me while visiting him in the hospital. He was his optimistic self. We said we loved each other, and he passed away soon after. Thank you, Melanie, for being our family representative at his Janazah.

Sometimes, things are just not meant to be. I know in my heart that he was the first man I loved for the sake of Allah; there was one more.

June 30, 2007

It was my retirement date and my birthday, so we had a party. It was so much fun with coworkers, family, and friends. After twenty-nine years, my career at DECCO was over. It had been a long run, but it was time to go. The timing was a few years early age-wise, but I wanted to travel, spend more time with my mom, and just relax. But there was still so much more in store. I continued to volunteer on union projects. One thing about the union, there is always work to be done, and they love volunteers. And I could always depend on Linda Allen to join in.

Linda was my coworker at DECCO, and we adopted each other for life.

April 2008

Geneva Wakeelah Abdullah passed away. She was ninety-two. It's really something when your mother is gone. Your life flashes to your earliest memory of her—she had always been beautiful, strong, feisty, and the backbone of our family. Our family had revolved around her. She loved Mu-min and loved her children—all five of us; she adored her grandchildren and lived to see a great-grandbaby. She was the oldest of eleven children born to Estelle and Frazier. She loved Allah and her Islamic community.

What do you do when the one person who has known you forever is no longer a phone call away?

September 2008

Our dear Imam Muhammad left us that September. It was a shock and once again unbelievable. You know how you can recall exactly where you were when certain things happen? I was visiting my mother-in-law when I heard the news on the radio. All I wanted to do was cry—another leader gone; there was such sadness for a while. I had always been so happy to be one of his followers. I pray that I can help make his future awesome!

May 2009

I lost my only sister, Fran. I don't have words to express what it's like when all your siblings have passed away, and it's just you left. It's a lonely feeling. You have your children, but it's not the same. All I can say is that Fran was the absolute best, and I was her little sister. So now, I was on a quest to find someone who knew me when I was little. Back to 421.

June 2009

My best friend whom I met when I was eleven, lost her battle with cancer: Franceno Muhammad. She was the one you could just tell everything to, and she would always give you wisdom. She left behind five wonderful young men, and I'm their Auntie!

The very next day my ex-husband, Clifton Earl Corbett Jr, made his transition. Clifton and I remained really good friends, and his family is my family, and we share Jessica—forever.

August 2010

My son John Jr. died. He had been attacked a year earlier and never recovered. This was an unbelievable time—so much loss, but his death was the worst. John was my firstborn and loved beyond belief. He got on my last nerve as children do, but you just want the best for them, and I couldn't imagine this loss. His passing has left a huge void in our family. I miss him every day. I'm thankful for my faith because it has gotten me through some rough years.

John was super smart, funny, loyal, and a rock when I was starting my single life. I pray that Allah will forgive his missteps and grant him Paradise. Ameen.

2011-2013

Imam Mubarak appeared at Masjid Wali Muhammad after being gone for more than twenty years. He was older but just as dynamic. We needed an Imam, but he wasn't chosen. So, he started a committee, and I joined. As I said before he was the type of Imam who liked to be out in the community, and he was making some strides. Our group invited the candidates for mayor, Duggan and Benny Napoleon, over to our spot. Adam Shakoor let us use his beautiful building for our committee meetings.

He also invited Troy Muhammad of the NOI. For me it was all about bridging folks together. We also took a busload of believers to Chicago to visit the NOI Temple and to the Mosque Cares. We prayed at the graves of Imam Muhammad and the Honorable Elijah Muhammad and his family members. We were also active in hosting a Ramadan session. It was a very exciting time. Sadly, Imam Mubarak had to leave us to be with family in LA for a while. We expected him to come back, and we kept in touch, but he ended up in Las Vegas where he became ill. I did see him in November 2018, and he made his transition in 2019. May Allah grant him Paradise.

June 2012

I was diagnosed with breast cancer. And looking back, I'm convinced that trauma will attack your body and cause it to fail you. My son's death and all that happened around that time was truly dramatic. He died from injuries he had received in 2011, and it was decided that his death should be prosecuted as an attempted murder. There was a trial, and unbelievable stuff started happening to our family. I'm the kind of person who minds her own business, but through this experience, I learned that trauma can seep in and destroy your life.

The next five years, I had a battle going on between radiation and a little pill that I was told I had to take for five years. The first pill left me unable to walk the distance of three houses down the street. Finally, my medication was adjusted, and I put my life in Allah's hands. Whatever His will was, I would accept. But I was going to fight as best I could. I had to ask, *What's going to happen to Iola/Ameedah?*

CHAPTER EIGHT

2015 to 2021

I Made the Five

My sister Fran died of breast cancer, and I thought that since we had different mothers, I didn't have to worry about that. The doctors always asked, "Did your mom have any cancer on her side of the family?" And the answer was always no. When I got my test back, I was shocked. Although our dad died of prostate cancer, I thought I was not at risk for cancer. My advice to everyone is to get your exams on time and be clear about your family's medical history.

When your body is failing, what can you do? I prayed and asked Allah to help me accept His will. That's always been my prayer. I try to do the work and ask God to help me. Before this, I didn't even take any medication but suddenly, I was on a five-year journey, and I didn't know what the outcome would be. Taking that pill was aggravating. Plus, that little pill cost me $500.00 for a thirty-day supply. I had to get a job to cover the cost of the medication.

And every year, mammogram time was the scariest. I dreaded opening up the report from the hospital, just praying for positive results. I'm so thankful that I got that examination every year because that's how they discovered the lump in the first place. And after five years, I got to ring the bell. I am pill free. I just learned I am cancer-free!

2020–2021 . . . and Grateful

In 2020, we had a pandemic to worry about; many people passed away from the virus. I lost close family members and friends. I stayed in the house for almost six months; it was kinda unreal, and I tried to get used to the new norm. When I go out, I'm masked and six feet away from other people. You can really reflect on life and death when you're alone and secluded. I've been praying and reading. May Allah have mercy on us all.

I haven't shared too much about John Sr. I was saving the best for last. John and I have shared five children. We lost our son, but life keeps going on. We see each other around the masjid, and when he needs a dish, I'm always willing. I know in my heart if I needed anything, he would come to my aid, and I would surely do the same for him. It's been over fifty years since we were married, but he's my friend. And over this last year, a lot of food baskets have been at my door, and a lot of meals have been shared. I thank Allah for people who care and are good friends.

I thank Almighty God that I made it to 2021. I'm humble and thankful. My family is amazing. My three daughters—Melanie, Jamillah, and Jessica kept me company on Messenger: We would have dinner, watch Jamillah cook dinner, share birthdays, and celebrate graduations. Tammy, my daughter-in-law (really my daughter), supplied so many meals. My oldest daughter hooked me up with a Zoom yoga class. My son Gamal did it all and is always just a phone call away. He might not answer, but he will call you right back.

The grandkids were awesome! Autumn did so much shopping for me; Angel called, came by, and we visited from her car—lol. Marshall and the rest of my out-of-state grandkids would all just check up on me. Raegan sent me Laffy Taffy's for my sweet tooth, and Cameron loved me from afar. My first grandson would text, FaceTime, and call. I had so much love. Thanks guys! So far, all the family, far and near, are doing well.

Grands and Great-Grands

Family

PS: I loved one other person for the sake of Allah, but I'll save that story for Volume 2 of my memoir.

MY DAG

My Dad's Story

What follows is my dad's story, which he wrote when he was seventy years old. Sister Tamra El-Amin gave it to me many years after my dad passed away. I don't even know how she got it or who typed it for him, but I was excited to read it. And when I did, all I could do was cry, and I mean that it was an ugly cry.

I wish he had shared it with me, and I wish I could have read it to my mom. After Almighty God, she was his biggest supporter. This helped me understand so many more things about him and his life growing up and why he gravitated so easily to the *Nation of Islam*. But in all, Allah knows Best.

Thank you, Daddy, for being an excellent role model.

IOLA "AMEEDAH" CORBETT

The Life of Mu-Min Abdullah
aka
Jessie Holmes, the Barber

1913–1986

Mu-Min Abdullah

With the Name of Allah the Gracious the Compassionate

My name is Mu-min Abdullah; my parents named me Jessie Holmes. I was born in Perry County, Mississippi about 21 miles south of Laurel, Mississippi. I was raised on several sawmill jobs.

I came to Detroit, Michigan when I was 24 years old. I came looking for my uncle whom I didn't know nor did he know me, but Allah Blessed me to find him. I didn't know at the time that Allah was God and the Creator of all things, the heavens and the earth. I was a Christian at that time and thought Jesus did all of that or he had a part in it anyway, because Jesus and the Holy Ghost were looking on when God created all of these things. There was nobody else around, so He let them see some of his Power and Speed. He did it in six days; then he rested on the seventh day. We were taught this in the church and on many sawmill jobs.

There were no schools for blacks; in some places, the parents would get someone that could read and write to teach us in the churches. When we were large enough to walk four or five miles, our parents would let us walk to the nearest one. Then we were really in trouble. We had to walk along the public gravel road where the white children came along riding in their school buses. While getting off or on the buses, they would throw rocks, hit and meddle with us, and call us all kinds of old black niggers and dirty names.

On some sawmill jobs they had what they called quarters, they would get the meanest white man they could find and make him boss over the quarters of the blacks. The company would provide these things:

- #1 a job to work every day except Sunday
- #2 to attend church.
- #3 trade at the company store, plenty of meat, all parts of the hog
- #4 the *Boarding House* where they would play music, sing, dance, drink whiskey, and gamble.

My parents were very righteous, and they would not let us go to the *Boarding House*. We went to church and Sunday school. I knew right from wrong when I was very young and I always wanted to do the right thing. I preferred treating people better than they treated me.

I learned to sing very well. I was the lead singer in the choir. The Methodist, Baptist, Holiness, Jehovah's Witness, Spiritualist, and the Israelites; you name it I was there for a little while.

I learned to cut hair when I was 14 and when I was 38 years old I had my own barber shop. During this time is when I learned about the Temple of Islam and met Brother George Bogans. He told me to come on around to the temple. He said, "You already a Muslim the way you talk and think. All you have to do is come on round to the temple," but I would not go. I thought I had already found the real thing in the Israelite faith. I would watch the Muslim sisters almost every day from my barber shop, passing on their way to the temple with their long dresses almost sweeping the ground. That didn't look good to me either because at that time I was the dead church going Negro Christian and I thought as they did. One of my friends told me that a nigger from Africa came over here and told those people that he was God and started a little old church and something went wrong. So, he left town and told them he was going to prepare a place for them and everyone to continue to believe in him. He said that on his return, he would take them back to heaven with him. Do you know, some of them believe he is coming back to get them.

One day, I was sitting in my barber shop reading the Bible when a little Muslim sister came in and introduced herself as Sister Ella D. X. She asked me if I was a preacher or reverend? I answered No, I was neither. She said, "Just about every time I pass by, you are reading that Bible. It's a good book, but you have to understand it." "Oh, I understand it very well. The Bible is what I like to read. I study this book." "What church do you belong to?" asked Sister Ella. "I belong to the Israelite." She said, "If I go with you to your church, will you go with me to the temple?" I paused, then I said, "Why did you put it that way? Sure, that would be no more than right. You go with me, I go with you." I could not make a promise and then refuse. So we planned for the next Sunday. Sister Ella met me at my restaurant the following Sunday morning at ten o'clock and we went to my Israelite Church. Bishop Tompkins was my pastor's name. After the meeting was over and on our way back to the restaurant, Sister Ella replied, "That sure is a preaching man. He can teach that Bible. I know the Bible is a good book, but you have to understand it."

I still remember her tender voice so well when she said, "If you want to, we still have time to go to the temple." I said, "Okay," so we went to the temple. This was to be my first visit to Muhammad's Temple of Islam.

The brother standing at the door welcomed us cordially. Just inside I saw a brother standing, whom I had seen many times before. He was very polite. Bro. Harold D.X. He came over and shook my hand and said, "Oh, here is the barber. Brother I know you have been to church but this is Muhammad's Temple, you will have to be searched." I said, "Ok." I knew I had nothing to hide. He said this is just our policy and we are always happy to have you come brother, no harm will come to you. Everyone has to be searched that enters our place of worship. You came at a good time, our visiting minister today is Malcolm X. I could hear the speaker on the inside, I wanted to hurry and get in to see who he was. Well, low and behold, this was the first time I laid eyes on and heard Malcolm X. This man Malcolm was a brave and powerful man. He kept his audience at his command. He said, "Elijah the prophet is in the land. God sent him to teach us things we don't know; we the Black American, so-called Negro. He has taught me to be his representative and he sends me here and there. Now, he is the leader and teacher, but he can't be everywhere. He said, 'you go and tell them what I said.' That is all I am going to tell because I know nothing to tell but what he taught me. He said we are the Original people of the Planet Earth. Nobody knew our beginning. We are the gods of the earth, the tribe of Shabazz. We have been in the hands of this wicked white man for four hundred years. This white man, he said, was the real Devil of the planet earth." If you were like me from Mississippi, it took very little persuasion because I knew very well the majority of them enjoyed giving Black people Hell. I am a witness.

Man, O man the whole congregation was spellbound. I learned more about the Bible, more about God, more about the Devil, more about religion, more about history, more about the government in which we live, and more about myself and my people. Truth that I could identify with; how to live a better and longer life. I learned more in three hours than I had in all of my 38 years of living. Elijah said, "Nobody wants us but God. The condition that this Devil has put us in sin, sin, sin." The job of cleaning us up was a tough one. He told us to put down the white man's way of life and there will be no more toil, no more strife. It is a pity and a shame that we don't give back the white man's names, his Bible, his religion, and his God. And you will see the good things Allah, the Creator will do for you.

All my life I had been seeking but never could I find any preacher or teacher who could satisfy my mind like Malcolm X. The only man of his kind, who could tell you so much in a short period of time. He even told us what we should and should not eat. Never the pig. Don't even touch his flesh. "No, don't even touch it, not to think of eating it." By this time, I was filled to the brim. Then he said, "I bring my talk to a close." I thought how I never could tire of him. I could have sat there all afternoon. "There is much more to learn." He said, "Just keep coming back. Now I will open up for questions." He remarked. After the dismissal and all were gathered outside talking, I wanted my wife, relatives and all to hear this good news coming from this great man. That we are the righteous and our time is at hand. All filled with pride, I felt rejoicing.

I was surprised to see my wife coming out of the temple with Sister Ella D. She was smiling as she made her way over to me as happy as she could be. We heard the good news together. Immediately, on our arrival home, we were so proud of the truth we had learned. We gathered up all our pure lard, pork chops, ham, bacon, pigtails and threw it all in the alley. Now we could drop the slave master's name, his teachings, and all his doings. We went back again and again. We asked questions and got answers about so many mysteries. That night as we tried to rest, we lay awake and talked most of the night. I thought to myself, *I am a Muslim and that is what I will be from now on.*

The resident minister was Minister Lemuel Hassan. Occasionally, he would teach Yacob's history. About this time, we decided to write our letter to reclaim our own religion Islam and worship Allah only and not baby Jesus nor the Holy Mother Mary.

It was sometime after that I went back to the Israelite Church and that was to try to get somebody out of there to go with me to the Temple of Islam. I went to almost every meeting. I wanted to learn all that I could. This truth was a new awakening for me. I truthfully can agree and understand when Imam W. Deen Muhammad refers to that time as the first resurrection. This was in 1953. So, many things were told to me about this little man named Elijah Muhammad. I had learned to love this little man so much. I became known as a sincere believer and follower and became completely interested and sorely meshed in service and propagation of Islam. I saw him as a righteous and holy person in the life that he lived. When I saw him face-to-face, he uplifted me spiritually and morally with his virtue and his grace. I wanted to be present at every place he went. Savior's Day Conventions, New York, Atlanta, Pittsburg, Philadelphia, we even went to Flint, Michigan.

We would knock at every door passing through. We sold the *Pittsburgh Courier*, *Herald Dispatch*, and the *Amsterdam News*. We sold to Negroes, Colored Folks, White Folks, and Jews. We would give many of these papers away if they would promise to read what Muhammad had to say. We made much progress and got on our feet. We started publishing our own newspaper, *The Muhammad Speaks*.

One day, Brother Wilburt and I was selling *Muhammad Speaks* newspapers in a black neighborhood as fast as we could. It was in the city of Monroe, Michigan, around forty miles outside of Detroit Michigan. A black man called the police and put them on our trail. The police picked us up and hauled us off to jail. When the police found out that he had goofed, he called Wilburt and said, "You and Jessie come with us; we are going to turn you loose."

My service to the propagation effort was so intense and my schedule so busy I could not give my attention to the restaurant. So I rented it out. Especially after knowing the truth, I could no longer run it anymore under the present conditions because most of my customers were eating Christians.

Finally, I meet the Honorable Elijah Muhammad. He looked different from all other men that I had seen and I never heard a man speak like this man before. I wanted to go down south. I wanted to tell all of my relatives and all my friends what I had learned directly or indirectly from this great man.

I took over my restaurant again and cleaned it up from top to bottom. I put in everything brand new, decorated and painted, and remodeled everything new again. We opened up under our new name *Shabazz Restaurant*. We became known throughout the nation from coast-to-coast.

My wife Geneva, learned how to cook the Muslim-style food. Sister Islam was living in those days, and nobody could cook pies like that sister. She made bean pie famous. We sold pies as fast as she could make them. When Minister Malcolm X would come to town, that would always be his first stop. He would bring the crowd from the temple to the restaurant. Also the Honorable Elijah and all of his sons, whenever they would come to Detroit, would stop by the restaurant. I was so happy. Now I had found what my heart desired; to be working and living among people who loved and cared for each other. We had a true leader, teacher, and guide. He loved his followers so much. He would teach us five or six hours at a time because we had been so poisoned with the white man's poisonous book. The King James Bible, it was a slave making book he would say. He always referred to the church as the icehouse. I remember one time he was teaching in a huge icehouse there in Chicago down on Indiana Avenue. He told us that "Some of you that's listening to my voice now will be living in the Hereafter." He said, "My job is to take you out of the Hellfire prepared for this wicked slave-making white man. And one will come after me and teach you the religion. He will make everything new. He will guide you into all truth." I didn't understand that at the time but we who truly believed in him and paid close attention to what he said, understand now very well. We see the one who came after him teaching the religion, making all things new and guiding us into all truth.

The Honorable Elijah Muhammad taught us that Allah came in the person of W. D. Fard and his true followers believed everything he said. We prayed to Fard thinking we were praying to Allah and many of our prayers were answered, I know mine were.

Now Allah has raised one from among us Imam W. Deen Muhammad to teach us the truth. Now we can sing that old song that says, "I am so glad I got my religion in time." All Praise is due to Allah, the One God, the Creator of everything and has power over everything. He created; He creates; He gives Life, and causes Death. He forgives us when we don't know any better. He has Mercy on us for He is the Most Merciful. He forgives us for believing Jesus was God. Oh yes, he even forgives us for believing Fard Muhammad was God. Allah has raised us from that state of death by giving to him a servant and has blessed him with knowledge far beyond the scope of the scientist of the present time. The one of whom I speak is none other than Imam Warith Deen Muhammad. He is my leader, teacher, and guide. It is he who has taught us Allah is One and Only, Absolute, and Muhammad is his servant and Apostle. (pbuh)

Imam Warith Deen Muhammad saved us from the hell that we had begun following in the *Nation of Islam* under the FOI. We were called Fruit of Islam when we should have been called stupid FOI fools of ignorance. We were better off in the days of the KKK. They did wear robes and hoods to let us know that they were our enemy, but they never harmed each other like the FOI; dressed alike but killed their Muslim brothers.

The Honorable Elijah Muhammad got sick and had to depend on others to help him carry on his work. This is when things began to grow from bad to worse. Insincere people, hungry for power and money, and infatuated with the power structure began to run things. Fakes and make believers, they would never tell us how sick the Honorable Elijah Muhammad really was. The true believers knew very little about what was going on.

When the news came over the radio that the Honorable Elijah Muhammad had died at 8:30 a. m., I was at the dentist having my teeth pulled. I could not hold back the tears. My wife was already in Chicago for the Savior's Day Convention where I would have been if I had not been sick. I didn't want to believe what I was hearing over the news. When I left the dentist, I went straight to the mosque. There were many like me perplexed, I didn't know whether I wanted to live or die. So, I prayed and prayed and Allah blessed me to think of what I had been taught that his son Wallace would be the next to rule after his father. Minister Lemuel Hassan used to teach us this.

Officially it was announced that his son Wallace was our new leader. Shortly after that announcement, my wife called me on the phone and told me the good news and that everybody was so happy.

I said, "All praise is due to Allah, I am happy too." I remember hearing the Honorable Elijah Muhammad say,

"No civilized people will follow a dead leader." When your leader dies, get you another leader, one that's alive like you are." Now we know that Allah is the only One that can give life and cause death. I have been in this community since 1953, following the leadership. I have seen many come and go. Allah be praised. I am seventy years old. I still feel good. I still cut hair. I still ride my motorcycle and I still sell papers. I started with the *Pittsburgh Courier* through to the *A. M. Journal* and by the help of Allah, I still give of that which He blesses me with. I thank Allah for my leader, Imam Warith Deen Muhammad.

I am Brother Mu-min Abdullah better known as Bro. Jessie Holmes, the barber.

W. D. Muhammad's teaching is appealing to righteous-minded people and if you are one, you will be inspired by his inspirational words. Then you will start moving in the right direction voluntarily. You will be doing what you want to do from the heart. Allah will let you enjoy your work because it will be good. Now you want good for yourself and everybody else that wants good for themselves. The Holy Quran is the book that has the guide for the righteous. Nobody in the world is working as hard as Imam W. D. Muhammad to bring the righteous together.

So, by the help of Allah we will become free of this present day wicked rule that rules over us today. Remember mean, evil, and wicked people exist because righteous people let them. Don't be left out. This is the work of Allah bringing the righteous together so we can be as good as we want to be. The better we become, the closer we will come together and by the help of Allah the one God who created the heavens and the earth, we will become the people that Allah invented for us to be.

As-Salaam-Alaikum

My dad with his motorcycle

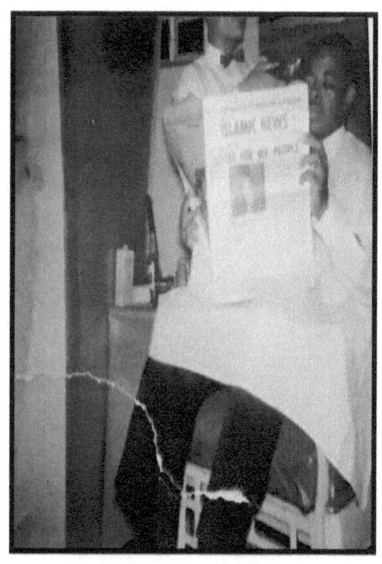

My dad at his barbershop

DOWN MEMORY LANE

Geneva Wakeelah Abdullah

Dad and Mom

Mom and Dad

Sister Josie Shah, Midwife at Temple #1

Bro. Joseph and Sis. Geraldine (at John C. Lodge)

FOI at Temple #1

Sister Marie Joshua and Alif Joshua

Muhammad Ali visiting Temple #1

School Days

IOLA "AMEEDAH" CORBETT

Having a White Party

Having a White Party

Sisters at the White Party

Brothers at the White Party

IOLA "AMEEDAH" CORBETT

University of Islam Alumni White Party

The World Community of Islam Identification Card

1978 World Community of Islam ID Card

A room full of sisters

A room full of sisters sponsored by Wisdom

Masjid Wali Muhammad and Guests Celebrating Temple #1's Historic Marker, 2019

Imam Munir Hanifa about to unveil our historic marker

GROWING UP MUSLIM

Historic Marker

Invited Guests

We welcomed Detroit Mayor, Mike Duggan

Masjid Wali Muhammad is historic.

Two of my favorite places: the beach and 16510

The Beach

16510

ABOUT THE AUTHOR

Iola Holmes Ervin Corbett was born in the North End of Detroit, Michigan. When she was very young, her dad and mom joined the *Nation of Islam* (NOI), and that's when this story, *Growing Up Muslim,* began. Iola's everyday life was shaped around many of the values she learned in her formative years.

Growing up, Iola's path crossed with some of the builders in the NOI like Malcom X, who probably made the biggest impression on her as a young girl. She also met Louis X (aka Louis Farrakhan) and The Honorable Elijah Muhammad. One of her real joys was being introduced to Imam W. D. Muhammad, who was the son of Elijah Muhammad. From the Imam, she received a broader view of worldwide Islam, a view she continued to follow.

Iola's education took place in the University of Islam and also Detroit Public Schools. In 1978, Iola became a member of the IAMAW (International Association of Machinists and Aerospace Workers). She was the first woman to be elected president of Local 82.

Iola is the mother of six children; she is a grandmother and a great-grandmother. For over 65 years, she has been a proud member of the Historic Masjid Wali Muhammad in Detroit, Michigan where she currently serves on the board.

Sometimes, there were crooked roads and bends in the road, but thankfully, Iola managed to stay on the straight path. Her many life experiences have inspired her legacy journey as shared in *Growing Up Muslim*.

www.ingramcontent.com/pod-product-compliance
Lightning Source LLC
Chambersburg PA
CBHW030156100526
44592CB00009B/309